KU-287-949

The Magic Box

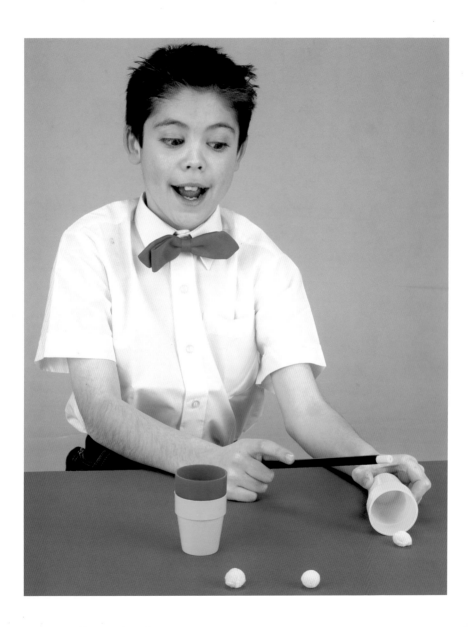

The Magic Box

Jon Tremaine

p

About the Author

Jon Tremaine has been a world class professional magician for more than 30 years. He is a member of London's Inner Magic Circle, and has been honored by them with a Gold Star, the highest award that a magician can receive. He has appeared on television, and traveled the world entertaining in top night clubs, hotels, and cruise liners. His specialty is close-up magic, the most difficult branch of magic to perform.

Jon has 30 non-fiction books to his credit covering subjects as varied as astrology, origami, balloon modeling, and backgammon, as well as magic.

This is a Parragon Book

This edition published in 2003

Parragon
Queen Street House
4 Queen Street
Bath BA1 1HE, UK

Copyright © Parragon 2001

Designed, produced and packaged by
Stonecastle Graphics Limited

Designed by Paul Turner and Sue Pressley
Photography by Roddy Paine
Edited by Philip de Ste. Croix

All rights reserved. No part of this publication may be reproduced, stored in a retrieval system, or transmitted in any way or by any means, electronic, mechanical, photocopying, recording or otherwise, without the prior permission of the copyright holder.

ISBN 1-40541-535-5

Printed in China

DISCLAIMER:
The tricks in this book are great fun but safety is very important.
• Always keep small items away from babies and young children.
• Children under 8 years of age can choke or suffocate on uninflated or broken balloons. Adult supervision is required. Keep uninflated balloons away from children. Discard broken balloons at once.
• The publisher and their agents cannot accept liability for any loss, damage or injury caused.

Contents

Introduction

Who is the most famous magician in the world? If you had asked me
that question a couple of years ago, I would have said David
Copperfield. Now, however, the undisputed World Champion
Magician is Harry Potter!

I know that David Copperfield is a live professional magician and that Harry Potter is only a figment of J.K. Rowling's vivid imagination, but the fact remains that the exploits of Harry Potter have captured the interest and imagination of children (and adults) the world over. Each year we look forward to his latest exploits and tricks and I, for one, am completely in awe of the beautiful magic that each book contains! I can't think of any character more magical.

As you learn to perform the super tricks in this Magic Box you must say to yourself: "What would the

trick look like if I could *really* perform magic – if I was a *real* wizard?"

Well – we know that it wouldn't look like a simple mathematical puzzle or a rhymed party trick of the type that is so popular with the average children's entertainer, would it? A wizard would just wave his magic wand, cast a magic spell and the "magic" would just happen! He wouldn't need to put something in a special box to make it disappear. He would just aim his magic wand at it and – zap – it would vanish. Do you get the idea?

I can't promise to turn you into a wizard. I will, however, show you how to perform some super tricks

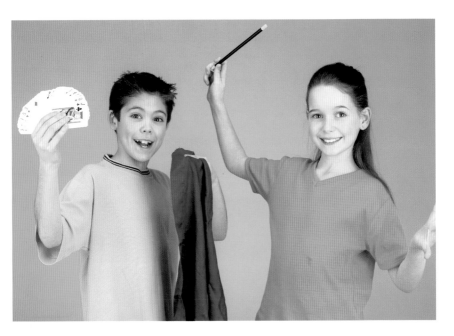

and teach you to present them as if they were **real magic**. Good magicians will fool you but not make you feel foolish. They will not insult your intelligence. They will suspend your beliefs for a while and lead you willingly into their exciting and entertaining world of magical make-believe.

All magicians have to start somewhere. Most start with a Magic Box like this one –

so press on and start practising. Practise in front of a mirror so that you can see what the trick looks like from the audience's viewpoint. Practise until you can almost do the trick in your sleep. Then (and only then) perform the trick for your friends. There are **five golden rules** that you must always follow:

1. Never tell anyone how you do your tricks. Keep your secrets *secret*!

2. Never repeat a trick to the same person on the same day. If someone knows *what* is going to happen, there is much more chance that they will find out *how* it happens.

3. Practise!

4. Practise!!

5. Practise!!!

SELF-WORKING CARD TRICKS

Time Out

Everybody loves card tricks. Each trick that follows is virtually self-working – requiring the minimum of sleight of hand – and yet they all contain a wonderful "magical punch".

The "methods" are cleverly disguised so that they appear inexplicable.

In this great trick you not only apparently read the mind of your assistant twice but also prove to her that you knew what she was going to think of before she thought of it!

What You Need
A pack of cards.
A sheet of thick A4 paper or card.
A black marker pen.

Preparation
Decide upon a "key" card. Let's say that you choose the Seven of Hearts. On one side of the paper boldly write:

You will
choose the
Seven
of
Hearts!

Your writing must not be noticeable from the other side – that's why we use thick paper (1).

Find the Seven of Hearts and on its back put a pencil dot at the top left and bottom right corners (2). These need only be faint as

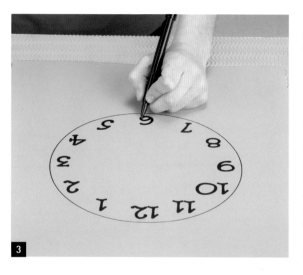

While you turn your back she must then remove the same number of cards *from the top of the pack* as the number she is thinking of (4) and sit on these cards. For example, if she thought of the number 3, she should remove three cards from the top of the pack and sit on them. If she thought of 4, she should remove four cards from the top and sit on them. When she tells you that she has done this, you turn around and pick up the remaining cards.

they are for your eyes only. Place this card in the *thirteenth* position from the top of the pack and you are ready to go.

What You Do

The pack of cards is on the table. Place the sheet of paper on the table, writing side down, without showing the writing. Draw a large circle on the paper and draw in the 12 numbers of a clock face (3).

Ask the spectator to think of any number from one to twelve – not to call it out, just to think of it.

5

Her jaw drops open in surprise as she tells everyone that you are correct. She removes the eight cards that she is sitting on to prove it.

"OK. Now have a peek at the card that is in the eighth position on the clock (6).

6

"There are twelve numbers around a clock – right?"

As you say this, you deal 12 cards from the top of the pack onto a separate pile, counting them out loud as you do this. This action reverses their order. Put the rest of the pack aside and pick up the packet of 12 cards. Now, starting at the one o'clock position, deal out a card beside each of the 12 numbers (5). Watch out for your secretly marked card. Remember its position but don't make it obvious.

From your point of view the "tricky bit" is over. Now you must act it up so that it becomes a mind-blowing trick. Say, for example, you have spotted your pencil-dotted card at the eight o'clock position. This is what you would say and do...

"You could have thought of any of the 12 numbers. That's true isn't it? Look at me. Just think of your number...don't say it...just think of it...You are thinking of...the number... eight! Am I right?"

"Don't show it to me – just think of it...You are thinking of...the...Seven of Hearts! Turn over the card and show everyone (7)."

7

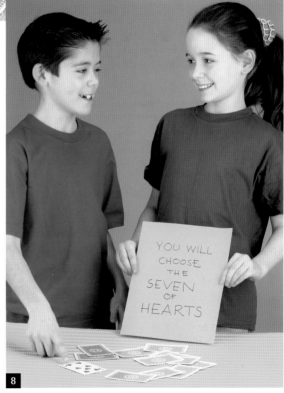

8

Afterthoughts

This is a self-working trick. The Seven of Hearts will always end up in the position that she thinks of.

Take time to learn the right words so that your instructions to the spectator are crystal clear.

You should get a nice round of applause at this point. Accept it modestly before you put in the final boot!

"Before we started I wrote you a little note. That note is underneath the clock. Would you please turn the clock over and read out aloud what I wrote!"

She reads out your message and your sensational card trick comes to a stunning conclusion (8).

YOU WILL CHOOSE THE SEVEN OF HEARTS

Lazy Aces

The spectator does all the hard work for you while you put your feet up and just direct the proceedings! She finds the four aces and won't have a clue how she did it.

What You Need
Just a pack of cards.

Preparation
Secretly place the four aces on top of the pack (1) and lay the pack on the table.

What You Do
Tell the spectator that you are feeling a bit lazy today and would like her to do a trick for you. You will tell her what to do.

First she must divide the pack into four roughly equal parts (2). Keep an eye on her as she does this and make sure that the quarter with the aces on top ends up in position number 4. If it isn't, casually move it to that position as you apparently tidy up the piles of cards.

Tell her to pick up pile number 1 and transfer

three cards – one at a time – from the top to the bottom of her packet (3). She must then deal one card onto the top of the other three piles in any order.

You now direct her to put the pile back on the table and pick up pile number 2. Again she should transfer three cards – one at a time – from the top to the bottom of the packet she is holding. Then deal one card on the top of each of the other three piles in any order she wishes before replacing the packet on the table (4).

You get her to repeat the procedure with piles numbers 3 and 4. The action of doing this to pile number 4 results in you getting rid of the three odd cards that were dumped on it and distributing aces to the top of each pile!

The dirty work is done. Now you must "sell" the trick...

"I chose you to do this trick with me because you look as if you would make a good poker player. You have done all the work for me. You cut the pack into four different piles and no one could know where you were going to cut. That's true, isn't it? You did all the dealing yourself and I haven't touched the pack once – have I? Let's see if I chose the right person – turn over the top card on each pile...!"

Watch her face as the four aces appear (5)!

Card Through the Table

In this quick, stylish trick a chosen card is pushed visibly through a solid wooden tabletop. This looks really magical when performed smoothly.

What You Do

Get the spectator to chose any card, remove it from the pack, and place it face upwards on the table in front of you (1).

While he is looking for his card (or before if you find it easier), secretly moisten the back of your right hand with saliva, water or any other liquid that comes to hand! When the card is in front of you, cover it with the back of your right hand and press down hard with your left hand (2).

Now remove your left hand, turning it palm up to show that it is empty and at the same time fractionally raise your right hand off the tabletop and draw it slightly towards your body. The moisture on the back of your hand will have caused the card to

stick to the back of your hand (3).

Pause for a silent count of three – then plunge your right hand beneath the table (4). Dislodge the card onto your lap (5) and then pick it up and bring the card out again – displaying it triumphantly for all to see (6)!

Afterthoughts
To get the full effect from this trick you must "believe it" yourself. If you don't apparently believe that the card has penetrated the table, you can't really expect the spectators to believe it too, can you?

It really did go through the table!

The Impossible Card Trick

This is probably my favourite card trick. I've been performing it for
more years than I care to remember. It is just as powerful now as it
was when I first came upon the principle and developed the trick.

What You Need
A pack of cards and a
dotted key card (see page 8).

Preparation
Place the key card in the
middle of the pack –
exactly the 26th card from
the top.

What You Do
Place the cards face
downwards in front of the
spectator at point A (1).

C B A

Have him cut off about
two-thirds of the pack
(over half) and place the
cards at point B (2).

He must now cut the pile
of cards at B approximately
in half and place these
cards at C (3). Your key
card will now be
somewhere in pile B.

Instruct the spectator to
pick up pile C and shuffle
the cards as much as he
likes (4). When he is
satisfied he must look at
and remember the card
that he has shuffled to the
top (5) – put it back on the

You must emphasize at this point that you have not touched or even seen a single card and that he has done all the cutting and shuffling himself. Get him to confirm that this statement is true.

top – and then place the whole of this packet of cards on top of pile B (6). His chosen card will now be on top of the combined B-C pile.

Now have him pick up pile A and shuffle them well before placing them on top of the B-C pile (7).

He can now give the cards as many complete single cuts as he wishes over and over again. All the cuts in the world will not alter the fact that his chosen card is now exactly 26 cards away from your key card – so although you don't know *what* it is, you do know *where* it is!

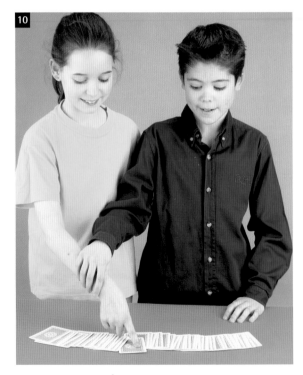

Take the pack from him and spread the cards face down across the table from left to right. Make sure that a small part of every card can be seen (8).

Ask the spectator to hold your right wrist. You say that you are going to attempt to receive "impulses" from him and thus find his chosen card (9). Extend your right index finger and, starting from the left-hand side, begin to move the finger slowly along the line of cards about two inches (5cm) above them.

When you spot the pencil dotted corner (your key card) count this as number

1, and continue to count the cards *silently* to yourself until you have reached the count of 26. Your finger will now be hovering over his chosen card.

Don't pick it up right away. Go a few cards further on – then retrace your steps. Hover over the cards in the vicinity of his card as though you are beginning to receive an "impulse" from the cards. Then drop your finger decisively onto the 26th card and pull it clear of the spread – still face down (10).

Have the spectator name his card out loud and then slowly and dramatically turn the card face up to show that your "impulse" was correct (11).

The "impossible" has been achieved. If it was "possible", we wouldn't bother to do it, would we!

Afterthoughts

If you reach the end of the line (the right-hand end) before you have reached the count of 26, merely continue the count at the left-hand end. His card will always be 26 cards away from your key card.

11

MONEY MAGIC

Voodoo Vanish

We are all interested in money. Tricks with coins and paper money appeal to people the world over. They are used to handling the stuff and so know what you should or should not be able to do with it. When you start to do the "impossible" with money, people sit up and pay attention – especially if you have borrowed the money from them in the first place!

It is not necessary to be a great "sleight of hand" expert to perform interesting and mystifying tricks. However, if you take the trouble to master this simple "vanish", you will be able to add a special sparkle to your tricks.

What You Need
A coin or any other small solid object.

What You Do
Hold the coin in your left hand as shown (1).

Your other hand travels forward to meet it – the right thumb going under and the right fingers over it (2).

3

Afterthoughts

Well, that's it. Simplicity itself – but remember to practise this simple combination of moves over and over again until they become second nature to you. You must act too – because if you don't appear to believe that the coin is in your right hand, you cannot very well expect your audience to believe it, can you?

Make as if to grab the coin with your right hand but as soon as it is hidden from the view of the spectators by your right fingers, let the coin drop secretly into your left palm (3).

Complete the grabbing motion with your right hand – closing it into a fist – and move the hand away as if holding the coin (4).

Do not move your left hand! Merely grip the hidden coin lightly with your second and third fingers. Your right hand is now slowly and dramatically opened – the coin has vanished!

4

The Vanishing Coin

This is "smart" magic! Several natural actions combine to create a beautiful mystery. Watch yourself perform it in your mirror.
"Mirror, mirror, on the wall.
This is the fairest coin vanish of all!"

What You Need
A coin which may be borrowed.
A clean handkerchief.
A jacket with an outside breast pocket.

What You Do
Display the coin held in the fingertips of your left hand at chest level and about two feet (60cm) away from your body. The back of your hand should face the audience (1).

Drape the handkerchief up and over the coin. Keep pulling the handkerchief over your left hand and towards your body (2) until the coin comes into view again. Your right hand comes to rest in line with your outside breast pocket.

Now repeat the above actions but as soon as your two hands come together, secretly grip the coin between your right finger and thumb – stealing it away under cover of the handkerchief (3).

Your right hand continues towards your top pocket as before. As soon as it reaches it, you let the coin drop unseen into the pocket (4).

The handkerchief has now cleared the left hand. The coin has disappeared. Show the audience that both your hands are empty (5) and pass the handkerchief out for examination.

Afterthoughts
This is a masterful piece of subtlety and you should practise the movements in front of a mirror until they all blend into one rhythmic motion. Have fun!

4

The Big "E"

So far we have made a coin vanish in a couple of different ways.
Now let's make a coin appear! You show both hands positively empty
and then proceed to pluck a coin from your elbow.

Preparation
Secretly tuck a large coin
into the back of your shirt
collar before you begin the
trick (1). You should be
seated at a table.

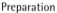

What You Do
Show both sides of your
hands to emphasize that
they are empty (2).

Pluck at your left elbow
with your right fingers as if
you are trying to remove
an imaginary "something"
from your elbow (3). You
have to bend your left arm
in order to do this – which
automatically brings your
left fingers directly over
the coin that is concealed
behind your neck!

Secretly remove the coin
from its hiding place. This
movement is covered by
the action of showing your

26

right hand to be still empty, having failed to produce anything from your left elbow (4).

Bend your right arm in the same way to expose your right elbow and immediately lower your left hand from your collar with the coin concealed and then "magically" produce it by plucking it from your right elbow (5)!

Display the coin (6). You can now make the coin vanish again by using any one of the methods that I have already described.

Boy Meets Girl

This is a cute little quickie and quite magical to look at. Two separate trombone-type wire paper clips suddenly jump into the air and, when they land, are seen to have become linked together! A marriage of convenience if ever I saw one!

What You Need
Two paper clips and a bank note (1). An ordinary piece of paper will do if you are broke!

Slide one of the paper clips over sections A and B (4). Make sure you get this right. Place the second clip over sections B and C as shown (5).

Hold the ends of sections A and C firmly and pull sharply in opposite directions (6+7). The two paper clips slide towards each other, join together and jump up into the air all at the same time (8).

What You Do
Fold the bank note in half along its long edge (2). Fold this into a "Z" formation as shown (3). Sections A and C are the same length and a little longer than section B.

28

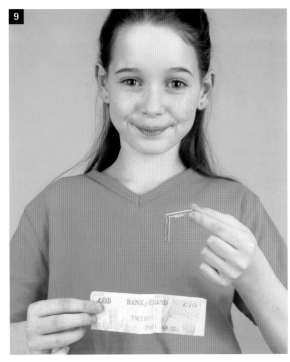

Afterthoughts

Make sure you place the paper clips in the correct positions! You could weave a story around this simple trick: Boy meets girl – they fall in love – money comes between them – but they finally get it together and get hitched (9). A little imagination is all you need!

Making Some Dough

You will have a lot of fun with this trick if, like me, you have an impish sense of humour! It is great for a restaurant situation or if you are invited as a guest to a smart dinner party or function. Have fun!

What You Need
A large coin and a bread roll (1)!

What You Do
When you are ready to perform, conceal the coin in your right fingers and pick up the bread roll in the same hand. The coin goes beneath the roll so you can hold the roll freely without the coin being seen (2). No one will

suspect that it is there because, at this point, nobody knows what you are going to do.

Hold the roll up and look at it intently. This will attract the attention of the other table guests. Shake the roll a few times beside your right ear. Pretend that you can hear something. Shake it by the ear of the person sitting next to you.

"Can you hear anything – No?"

Shake it beside your own ear again – then seize the roll at opposite ends with your thumbs on top.

Bend the ends of the roll *up* to crack the crust on the bottom of the roll (3).

Secretly push the coin up into the crack (4).

"I wonder if there are any more like that?"

Watch everyone grab for their rolls – it's hilarious!

Afterthoughts
If you are "in funds" you could do the trick with a folded banknote. It works just as well!

Now bend the ends of the roll *down* to crack the roll at the top. Keep the bottom parts pushed together to stop the coin falling out.

Put your thumbs into the crack to continue the breaking process and suddenly the edge of the coin will pop into view (5).

"Oh! My goodness! Look at this!"

Now, very slowly and openly, reach into the roll with your right index finger and thumb and very delicately remove the coin from the centre of the roll (6).

POCKET TRICKS

The Slave Bangle

As the name implies, the following series of tricks can be easily carried in your pocket and as a result can be performed at the drop of a hat. You will be the life and soul of the party!

This is a very "different" sort of a trick. Its strength lies in its sheer simplicity. Always remember that the method of achieving a trick is not important. Only the final effect on the audience should be considered.

What Happens

A spectator ties your wrists with a piece of string. She hands you a small bangle, having first examined it. You turn your back on her for a split second and when you face her again the bangle is threaded on the string – yet your wrists are still securely tied.

What You Need

Two identical bangles. (The spectators are only ever aware of one bangle!) A three-foot (1m) length of string. You must also wear a jacket.

Preparation

Slip one of the bangles over your right hand and push it up your jacket sleeve until it is out of sight (1). You are now ready to perform.

What You Do

Pass out the visible bangle and the string for minute inspection and then have the spectator tie each end of the string to your wrists leaving plenty of slack

32

between them (2). Make a big thing of this. It is important that the spectator realizes that you cannot possibly release your wrists.

Pick up the bangle with your right hand (3) – then quickly turn your back on the spectator.

As soon as your back is turned, put the bangle in your inside jacket pocket (4) and, *at the same time*, pull the hidden bangle out of your right sleeve – over your right hand (5) – and leave it hanging suspended from the string between your hands (6).

Turn around – the miracle is done (7).

Afterthoughts
You should be able to complete this series of actions in about three seconds. The faster you do it, the more impressive the trick is.

Occasionally someone will ask you to take the bangle off again. You can do this by reversing the process: turn your back and with your left hand pass the bangle along the string – over your right hand – and push it back up your right sleeve. As soon as the bangle has cleared your hand, reach into your inside jacket pocket and remove the other bangle. Turn around and hand the bangle to the spectator!

The Broken and Restored Match

This is a very good trick but it is quite well-known. I will first describe the classic method of performing it, and then my follow-up where you repeat the trick using a completely different method that will fool everybody! It is always nice when you are able to fool the pants off a "know-all". I'm sure you know the type – the person who has an answer for everything. Nothing is beyond her powers to explain – or so she genuinely believes. You are just about to shoot the legs from under her!

What You Need
A pocket handkerchief with a wide hem.
Two matchsticks.

Preparation
Hide one of the matchsticks by pushing it into the hem of the handkerchief (1). You will find this very easy to do due to the way handkerchiefs are sewn

together. The spectators think that only one match is used.

What You Do
Spread the handkerchief on the table and place a matchstick on its centre (2).

Fold the corners into the centre covering the match. The corner with the hidden match is folded in last (3). Hang on to this corner and pick up the bundled handkerchief – turning it over in the same action.

Ask the spectator to feel that the match is still there. Guide her hand to your hidden match. Everything looks and feels normal to her (4).

Now request that she break the match through the cloth – she can snap it into several pieces if she wishes!

When this is done you must say a magic spell – wave your hand over the bundle (5) – then shake the handkerchief out. The broken match drops into view fully restored (6). Your hands are empty. Show your spectator both sides of the handkerchief before you return it to your pocket.

Broken and Restored Match Revisited

I learned to do the last trick when I was five years old, and that was many, many years ago I assure you! The following method of performing the same trick enables you to repeat it immediately and this time you will fool even those "in the know"!

Instead of hiding the other match in the handkerchief, you conceal it in the lining of your tie (7)! Another "killer" feature of this version of the trick is that you also borrow the handkerchief!

What You Do

First get somebody to mark the match with a pen to emphasize that only one match is going to be used.

Proceed exactly as before up to the point where you pick up the bundled handkerchief. All you have to do now is secretly to take the end of your tie up into the centre of the handkerchief. This will never be noticed because the cover from the handkerchief and your hands is very good.

Have the spectator break the match (in your tie). Work your magic (8), then shake out the handkerchief. Your tie drops back into place and the original match falls to the table – fully restored (9)! Your hands are empty and the handkerchief can be minutely examined.

Dotty Spots

I love tricks that can be performed with ordinary objects. If you can make magic happen with them, the effect is always very strong. Dotty Spots is great for a dinner party situation. Paper dots that are stuck on the blade of a knife disappear and reappear at the will of the magician (that's you)!

What You Need
A table knife – a butter knife is the easiest size to use.
A paper napkin.

What You Do
Prepare by tearing off four identical circles of the paper napkin. Moisten them and stick two on each side of the knife blade. Make sure that both sides look identical. Hold the knife in your right hand as shown (1).

"You will notice that I have got two spots on this side of the knife and..."

Turn the knife over to show the other side by just turning your wrist. Do not move your arm (2).

"...and two spots on this side."

Twist your wrist back again so that the knife returns to its original position.

"Now, if I wipe off the spots..."

Put your left thumb over the spot nearest the handle and apparently put the ball of your first finger over the spot on the underside (3). Pull your thumb back towards the left – peeling off the top spot and apparently pulling off the spot that lies directly beneath it too. Repeat this with the spot furthest from the handle (4).

Crumble the little pieces of napkin into a ball and

Now turn your wrist back again and at the same time pull *backward* with your thumb and push *forward* with your first finger (7). You have shown that the knife now has no spots on either side when in reality you have none on the visible side and two spots underneath the blade. We call this the Paddle Move. Practise this in front of a mirror so that you can see exactly how it looks from the front.

discard them. The spectator will think that all of the dots have been removed.

Now we do the clever bit! Twist your right wrist over to show the other side of the knife – like you did before – but at the same time move the tip of your thumb *forward* and the ball of your first finger

backward. This has the effect of revolving the knife and showing the same side of the knife twice (5+6)!

The larger action of turning the wrist disguises the smaller action of your thumb and finger as they secretly twist the knife handle.

"Now I'll show you some magic..."

Do the paddle move to show that the knife is now clean on both sides (8). In reality you still have two spots on the underside.

"Now watch closely..."

Pass your left hand over the knife blade in a downward direction and under cover of your hand revolve the knife between your thumb and finger. The spots are now seen to be back on the knife again (9). Do the paddle move and show that two spots have returned to the other side too (10)!

"They've all come back again. Now that is magic!"

Put your thumb on the spot nearest the handle and peel it off (11). Don't pretend to peel one from the underside this time.

"The strange thing is that if I take a spot off one side..."

Do the paddle move (12).

"...the spot on the other side vanishes."

Peel off the last spot (13).

"I'll take the last spot off..."

Show both sides of the knife minus all spots (14).

"Now please would you pass me the butter so that I can eat my bread roll!"

Afterthoughts
Please practise the paddle move until it becomes second nature to you. Magicians use this subtlety in a variety of tricks.

The Cut and Restored String

It is always nice to perform tricks with everyday objects – things that the audience are very familiar with. They think they know what you can do or cannot do with the object, so when you do the impossible with it, the effect is quite startling! This is just such a trick.

What You Need
A drinking straw.
A length of string that is thin enough to be threaded through the straw.
A pair of scissors.

Preparation
Secretly cut a three-inch (8cm) slit along the centre on one side of the straw (see diagram above).

What You Do
Pick up the straw with the secret slit facing your own body and unseen by the audience. Thread the string through the straw (1).

Fold the straw exactly in half and during this process

44

pull down on both ends of the string. The centre part of the string will come through the slit in the straw and this portion should be carefully covered by your left thumb and index finger (2).

Pick up the scissors and snip through the centre of the straw (3).

The two halves of the straw can now be openly displayed (4). The straw (and apparently the string too) has definitely been cut in half.

Butt the two cut ends together again and pull on one end of the string (5). Magically it comes away fully restored (6)!

Afterthoughts

Casually put the two cut halves of the straw away in your pocket. You could, if you wish, previously prepare another straw by just cutting it in half and put the two pieces in the same pocket. You could then exchange the slit ones for the unslit ones and your secret method would remain undiscovered!

Only do this exchange if the genuineness of the straw is questioned. This is a Cut and Restored String trick not a Cut and Restored Straw trick after all!

4

Colour-Changing Balloon

This trick really makes an impact! A very noisy one! The colour change is instant and most effective.

What You Need
Two balloons of different colours – say one red and one blue.
A drawing pin.
A small blob of Blutack.

What You Do
Insert one balloon inside the other (1). Blow up the inner balloon and knot the end. Blow some air into the

outer balloon so that there is air space between the two balloons and tie this one off too (2).

Stick the drawing pin onto your thumb using the Blutack (3).

3

When you are ready to perform the trick, hold the balloon(s) by the knotted end. Count to three and then burst the outer balloon with the drawing pin. There will be a loud pop and the balloon will instantly change colour (4)!

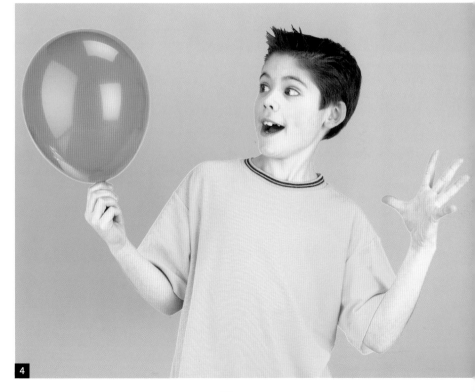

4

Penetrating Pencil

Once again everyday objects are used to perform a trick. The props
can be borrowed and the effect is very cute. It is a completely
impromptu trick – nothing needs setting up beforehand – so you can
perform it anywhere.

What You Need
A pencil or pen.
A handkerchief.

What You Do
Close your right hand into
a fist and then cover it
with the handkerchief (1).
Under cover of the
handkerchief secretly open
up your fist into a "C" shape
– as if you were holding
a glass.

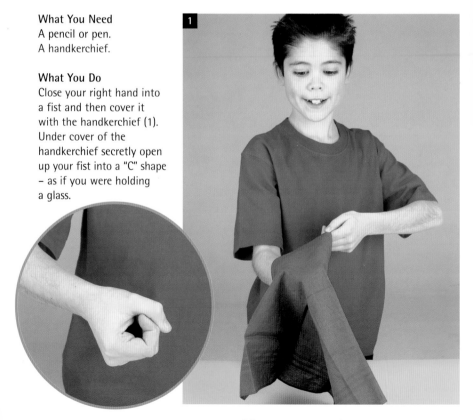

This action will have created a secret tunnel that the folds of the handkerchief now cleverly conceal. Take a pencil and push the blunt end a little way into the hole. Display it in this position as you attract the attention of the spectators (3).

Apparently you now use your left thumb to depress a hole in the handkerchief by pushing material into the well of your right fist. That's what it looks like! What actually happens is that you push your thumb *sideways* into your fist well, dragging some of the handkerchief with it (2). Once the thumb is in, you close up your right fist – then remove your thumb and push it in and out of the well again a couple of times, this time from the top!

You now unsuccessfully attempt to push the pencil through the handkerchief a couple of times.

"It would probably be easier if I put the pointed end in first!"

Take the pencil out – turn it around – and put it back in the hole, sharpened end first (4).

"Now – watch!"

Relax the grip of your right hand on the pencil and it will sink slowly and mysteriously into your fist.

Delicately reach under the bottom of the handkerchief and pull the pencil free (5). It has apparently passed through the centre of the handkerchief (6)!

Turn your right hand over to place the handkerchief on the table and your tunnel will have disappeared.

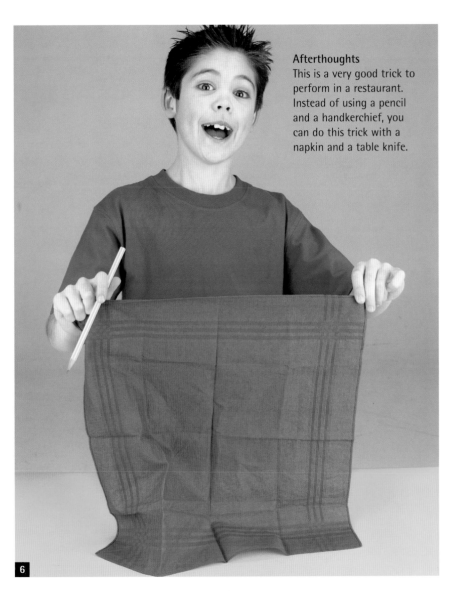

Afterthoughts
This is a very good trick to perform in a restaurant. Instead of using a pencil and a handkerchief, you can do this trick with a napkin and a table knife.

6

CLASSIC MAGIC

The Famous Cups and Balls

Classic magic tricks are those that pass the test of time. They fool people today just as much as they fooled people when they first saw the light of day. The next two tricks can justifiably be called "classics".

When we look through the magical archives, we find that the earliest known magician was called Dedi. He lived 2,500 years ago in Egypt and it is reported that he was extremely fat. He would binge on 500 loaves of bread and a shoulder of beef and drink about 100 pints of beer every day. The Cups and Balls is a version of one of his tricks and is just as good today as it was all those years ago.

What You Need
Three cups.
Four coloured balls.

Important
Four balls are used in this trick although the spectators think that you are using only three.
This is our secret (1).

Preparation
We will call the three cups A, B and C. Stack the cups together after secretly

loading a ball in the centre cup, B. The other three balls are in cup A.

What You Do
Lift up all three cups together and pour the three balls out onto the table.

Pull off cup C with your right hand (2), turn it over, and place it smartly onto the table – mouth downwards (3).

Pull off cup B and place this mouth downwards next to cup C (4). Keep the mouth of the cup pointed away from the spectators. If you do it smartly enough, you will be able to do this without the secret ball that it contains being seen. Turn cup A over and place that next to the other two (5).

Place a ball in front of each cup. Put the ball that is in front of cup B on top of it (6). Cover it with cups C and A (7). Tap the top (8) and lift up the stack of cups to show that (apparently) the ball that you placed on top of cup B has penetrated the cup and now rests upon the surface of the table (9).

Lay the three cups out again with cup C (which has a ball in it) going over the ball that has just appeared in the middle of the table. There are now two balls under the centre cup and one in front of each of the others (10–13).

Place one of the visible balls on top of the centre cup (14) and cover it with cups B and A (15). Tap the top and lift the cups to show that there are now *two* balls lying beneath the stack (16).

Again reset the cups on the table with the centre cup going over the two balls that have apparently penetrated the cup (17).

There are now three balls under the centre cup, although the audience will only be aware of two. Place the last visible ball on top of the centre cup (18) and assemble your stack all over again (19).

Tap the top and lift up the stack of cups. All three balls have apparently penetrated through the solid cups (20). Amazing!

The Magic Ball and Vase

This Magic Ball and Vase trick was invented over 100 years ago and was first made in boxwood. The surviving vases are now collectors' items. The plastic version that you can find in most magic shops, however, works just as well. The "instructions" that accompany this trick are usually terrible, so it is a pleasure for me to have the opportunity to write some proper instructions so that you may learn and enjoy performing this wonderful trick.

The Apparatus
The Ball and Vase comes in four parts that fit together. It consists of the lid, a half-ball shell which has an extra rim around it that matches the colour of the lid and base, a plastic ball, and the base (1).

The basic function of the apparatus is the option that it gives you either to show the vase empty or to show that it contains a ball – even though the ball has been openly removed. To acquaint yourself with this function, first take out the

ball and reassemble the other three parts. To show that the vase contains a ball, lift the lid by gripping the pointed top. This shows a ball in the vase. You are actually seeing the top of the half-ball shell. Put the lid back on. This time lift the lid *and* the half-ball shell together by gripping the vase by its sides. The vase is now shown empty.

What You Do
Assemble all four parts together (2). Pick up the vase in your left hand and with your right hand lift off the top *and* the half-ball section to display the real ball (3). Tip the ball out onto the table (4). Put the top and shell back on top

1

2

4

5

3

of the base and set it down on the table.

Pick up the ball and put it in the top pocket of your jacket (5). Say that you will make the ball disappear from your pocket and reappear inside the vase again. Make a few "magic passes" (6) – then reach across and lift off the lid by its pointed tip.

6

The "ball" is back in the vase (7)! They really see only the shell. Put the lid back on (8).

Say that you will make the ball disappear from the vase and reappear back in your pocket. Make some more magic passes (9)– utter a few magic words – then lift off the top of the vase by its sides to show that it is empty (10). Reach into your top pocket to remove the ball (11) or, better still, get a spectator to do it for you!

Afterthoughts

While the spectator is removing the ball from your top pocket, you can palm off the shell and secretly drop it into your pocket. If I'm sitting at a table, I will just let the shell drop unseen onto my lap! The vase can now by passed out for minute examination and your "secret" will be intact. In the hands of a sleight-of-hand expert this trick can take on almost miraculous proportions. Please play about with the apparatus. See how you can improve your performance of the trick by doing a Voodoo Vanish of the ball.

Another variation is to have the ball secretly concealed in your left fingers. Pick up the vase with the same hand. With your right hand lift off the lid by its pointed top to show that the ball is inside. Put the top back on. Give the vase a squeeze with your left hand and then let the palmed ball drop onto the table. Lift off the lid (this time by its sides) to show that the vase is now empty. The ball has apparently penetrated through the vase!

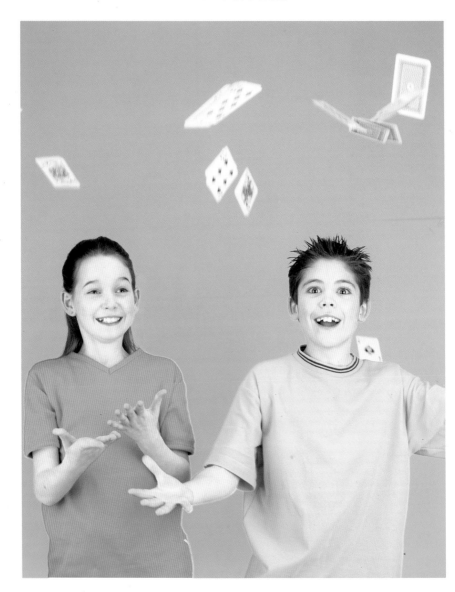